IN AMERICA'S SHADOW

IN AMERICA'S SHADOW

Story by KIMBERLY KOMATSU and KALEIGH KOMATSU

Foreword by KEVIN STARR

Essay by MITCHELL T. MAKI

TO THE SPIRIT OF MORE THAN ONE HUNDRED TEN THOUSAND
JAPANESE AMERICANS WHO WERE PLACED BEHIND BARBED WIRE,

BECAUSE THEY FACED DISCRIMINATION AND STRUGGLE
WITH DIGNITY AND PERSEVERANCE
BECAUSE THEY DID NOT LET ANYONE TAKE FROM THEM
THEIR HUMANITY
OR
THEIR SPIRIT
FOR THIS WE ARE GRATEFUL
FOR THIS WE ARE PROUD

TO THE NISEI OF THE 442ND REGIMENTAL COMBAT TEAM,
THE 100TH INFANTRY BATTALION, AND THE MILITARY INTELLIGENCE SERVICE,

FOR THEIR COURAGE AND FIGHTING SPIRIT
WHO ENDURED
WHO SACRIFICED
WHO FOUGHT AND GAVE THEIR LIVES
BECAUSE THEY BELIEVED IN
A BETTER AMERICA
THAN THE ONE THEY HAD KNOWN

A PROJECT OF THE CALIFORNIA CIVIL LIBERTIES PUBLIC EDUCATION PROGRAM

This book is made possible in part by the California Civil Liberties Public Education Program, whose purpose is to leave a legacy of remembrance so that future generations will understand the Japanese American internment experience.

Published by Thomas George Books
P.O. Box 861853, Los Angeles, California 90086

TO THOSE WHO HAVE MADE THE JOURNEY POSSIBLE

FOREWORD

Over the past four decades, literature written for children and young adults has increased significantly in its complexity of themes. Young adult literature especially, both fiction and non-fiction alike, has shown itself to be notably creative and courageous in presenting its young adult readers with stories of tragedy and suffering, abuse and injustice, as well as the bright side of life. And now comes this book written by two young Japanese Americans, which encourages its young readers to grapple with one of the most tragic and intractable episodes of American history: the internment of Japanese Americans during the Second World War without regard to their feelings, citizenship, or constitutional rights.

This grave injustice remained for a number of years a non-discussed experience akin to a taboo. It could be remembered, that is, in sorrow and pain—but it could rarely be talked about, and then only in private. Nearly forty years ago, however, the Japanese American community began increasingly to talk about what happened—and to ask their fellow Americans to meditate upon what had been done to loyal citizens of this Republic, together with a generation of equally loyal non-citizens of longtime residence, strictly on the basis of their race. This conversation has taken the form of histories, symposia, public discussions, even remuneration (however token, compared to the losses) by the federal government to former internees.

And now, in both prose and photographs, thanks to IN AMERICA'S SHADOW by Kimberly Komatsu and Kaleigh Komatsu, this conversation, this dialogue, this act (frequently painful) of memory, comes to the world of literature for young people. Through sensitive prose and in telling photographs, young readers are challenged in this book to re-experience for themselves that sense of baffled and betrayed love of country that so characterized the internment. Thanks to the miracle of photography, moreover, young readers are also being encouraged to visualize for themselves what the internment looked like, from start to finish, and of equal importance to see for themselves just exactly who were the people—in terms of their origins, their immigration, their settlement in the United States, and their love of country—who were so betrayed in their hopes for a respected and stable American identity.

This is a beautiful book, but it is also a painful book because it tells a painful story. And yet this is a book that refuses to allow pain to turn itself into a crippling bitterness. This is a book that encourages its young readers to struggle towards hope, to regain a sense of the future, just as an entire generation of Japanese Americans was forced to regain hope for itself and for the nation that had betrayed them. Many internees sacrificed their lives in far-flung battlefields. Others remained steadfastly loyal to their country behind barbed wire. Young people reading IN AMERICA'S SHADOW will be challenged to grasp and meditate upon a most complex message indeed: namely, that in the midst of tragedy and injustice, nobility and family values managed to prevail and love of country engendered the beginnings of reconciliation and forgiveness.

KEVIN STARR

State Librarian of California

T H E

J O U R N E Y

I remember how the harsh winds of Manzanar

came, and with its fury swept us from our

home. I remember you said that our stories

were all that we had in this world. They

keep us strong through the bad times and help

us strive for something more during the good times.

They are all that remain of us even when we are gone. I have never forgotten

the promise I made as a child. I have never forgotten how the story begins . . . . .

Aiko

MANY, MANY YEARS AGO, WHEN STREETS WERE DIRT ROADS, WHEN WAGON WHEELS TURNED AND BUFFALO ROAMED, AND things were very different, my grandfather and grandmother left their home in Japan to come to America. Their hearts longed for adventure.

Grandfather and Grandmother sailed across a vast, sparkling blue sea made from their hopes and dreams and journeyed to find America.

They dreamed of building a grand and magnificent hotel. Perhaps it would be the grandest one in all of the West.

To the wind they tossed uncertainty, for there were too many dreams to be dreamed, too many winding roads awaited the sound of their footsteps. So they listened to their hearts and followed the clouds to a place called Hanna, Wyoming.

Outings with plumed hats and pocket watches filled spring days, while spring evenings were filled with the many colors of a lavender sunset. Their backyard was the Rocky Mountains, their front yard the Great Plains. Grandfather and Grandmother were very, very happy.

But sometimes things do not work out as you plan, and no one can predict that hard times and struggle lay ahead.

For one fleeting moment, Grandfather and Grandmother thought of returning to Japan, but this country called America was so beautiful that the very thought of leaving made their hearts ache.

My grandfather and grandmother had come to America to build a hotel, they did not know that they would end up building America with their stories.

"That was a very long time ago, dear Aiko," Grandfather says to me. I wish I could stay here in our house forever with my grandfather and his stories, but now we must pack because it is time to go.

The United States is in a terrible war, and the government has issued Executive Order 9-0-6-6. This means that we will have to leave everything behind and go live in a place called an internment camp. All we can take is what we can carry, and what we can carry is all that we will have left in this world.

I am only ten years old, but it is still hard for me to pack my whole life in one suitcase.

People are angry and filled with hate, they are looking for someone to blame. They refuse to realize that we too are Americans.

"Do not be afraid," Grandfather says to me, "9-0-6-6 is only a number and nothing more, it cannot take away who we are." But I know it is a number that will change our lives forever.

The house we are leaving behind is filled with the memories of Grandfather's journey: faded photographs, letters filled with enough hope for even the saddest day, buffalo that stay silent in stone, an old cigar box where a single eagle's feather is kept. These are the gifts my grandfather was given on his journey to find America. A lifetime of things that cannot be counted or measured. A lifetime of things that should remain with Grandfather, but we cannot take everything with us, only what we can carry.

I wonder if it is hard for Grandfather to decide what he will take with him and what he will leave behind. Without these things I wonder if it will be hard for Grandfather to remember his journey that began so long ago.

But Grandfather packs none of these things. His family *keizu*, an ancient scroll on which the stories of his ancestors are written, is what Grandfather brings with him. He has kept this close to his heart and always will, like a promise you keep forever.

Grandfather brings with him one more thing, but it is something that he cannot pack in a suitcase. It is something he can only hold within his heart.

Within his heart Grandfather holds the belief that America is still a good place. Faith in this country, in spite of what has happened, is what Grandfather brings to remind him of where we are headed. His *keizu* he brings to remind him of where we have been, and that is all he needs.

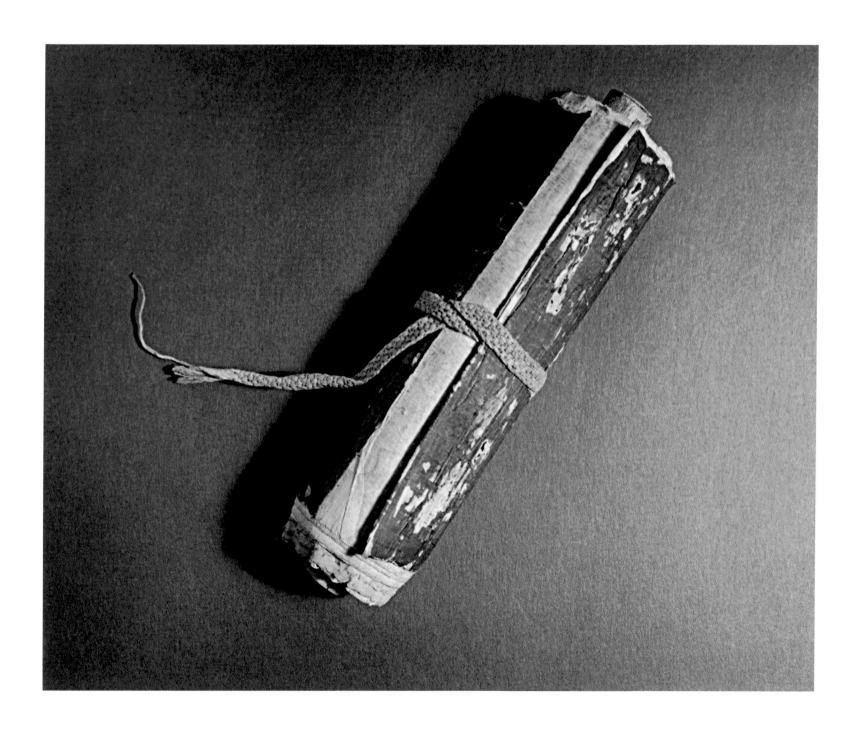

We ride one last time in our car to the train station, Mom, Dad, Grandmother, Grandfather and me. The city stands empty with boarded up windows and doors, like a ghost town left lifeless without a soul.

Houses with fields of promises, where Japanese American families once lived, have quickly become bidding grounds where years of hard work and struggle are bought at a cheap price.

No one hesitates, eagerly they wait to profit from injustice.

When we arrive at the train station there are many other families there. Silently they stand with their suitcases and bundled packages. Where we are going, we cannot take the new car my mother and father worked so hard to buy, so we give it to the stranger that drove us here.

Our rights as Americans have been taken away, no one will listen, no one cares. The ones who do not call us names look the other way. They pretend they do not see, they pretend they do not hear.

I want to right this wrong. I want to believe in America. I want to do something for those who have lost so much. But it feels like there is nothing in the world I can do to change what is happening.

"Remember what you see, and listen to the voices around you," Grandfather says. "One day you will find the part you play in this, one day you will find a way to help us." But I still do not yet know what it is I can do, so I do as Grandfather says, and I look around and listen.

I hear no bitter words in anyone's heart. I see no gritted teeth or clenched fists. I see people who had worked hard to make this country a better place, their heads held high with dignity and grace. I see Americans.

Inside the train the shades have been pulled down tight. It is dark now except for the rays of sunlight that somehow find their way through. I cannot look out the window to see where we are going, or see what waits for us there, so I sit quietly and think.

I think about how angry and hateful people are to us when we have not done anything wrong. I think about how unfair things are, and I want to run away from it all.

"Grandfather, please tell me a story," I ask, in a voice as quiet as hope lost in a storm. Grandfather hears me, he always understands, and in his eyes I can see that he is remembering.

"I will tell you a story," Grandfather says. "It is about the past. A time when the great rumble of the buffalo could still be heard. A time very far away from today."

When miles and miles of track lay ahead of him, like thread weaving itself in and out of the land, my grandfather traveled the railroad.

That was when he was not much older than a boy, before he even came here with Grandmother. His brave and free spirit set out to find the beauty that was hidden in all things.

When the West was wild and there were still places that never knew the footsteps of man, my grandfather walked this land.

Grandfather made many friends and listened to their stories.

One night, beneath a sky of painted ink, with a fire blazing bright, an old, wise man, who had lived countless moons, shared with Grandfather words of days gone by. Their shadows danced, flickering against the wind.

And when the wind rustled through the tall prairie grass, the old man and Grandfather sang the songs of their childhood. They wandered through memories, traveling far to forgotten places, until their journey together had made them a part of one another's story.

Though the old man and Grandfather had come from worlds apart, though their lives had been very different, they had found that their hearts were the same. For they both shared the spirit of the wild that would forever whisper in their ear.

Into the night their voices echoed, until the first light of dawn was beginning to break. The old man knew that the time had come to say goodbye.

"Your journey will be long, your footsteps will go far," the old man said to Grandfather. "This land is a good place. It is a place of promise. But sometimes even promises are broken, and you will have to find your way through. You will have to look beyond the broken promises to see again."

Grandfather and the old man were both on a journey, but it was Grandfather's journey that was just beginning.

And as the last embers of the fire flickered and burned out, the old man said goodbye.

"I have left most of my things behind," Grandfather says. "But I have not left everything. My stories and my memories I will keep with me always."

I thought about all of the places Grandfather had visited and all of the people he had met in his life. Maybe one day I will begin my own journey.

I listened to the steady rattle of the train as it made its way into the night. For one moment before I fell asleep, I knew that I was safe.

IT IS A STRANGE AND SAD FEELING TO WAKE UP ONE DAY and realize that you are not free.

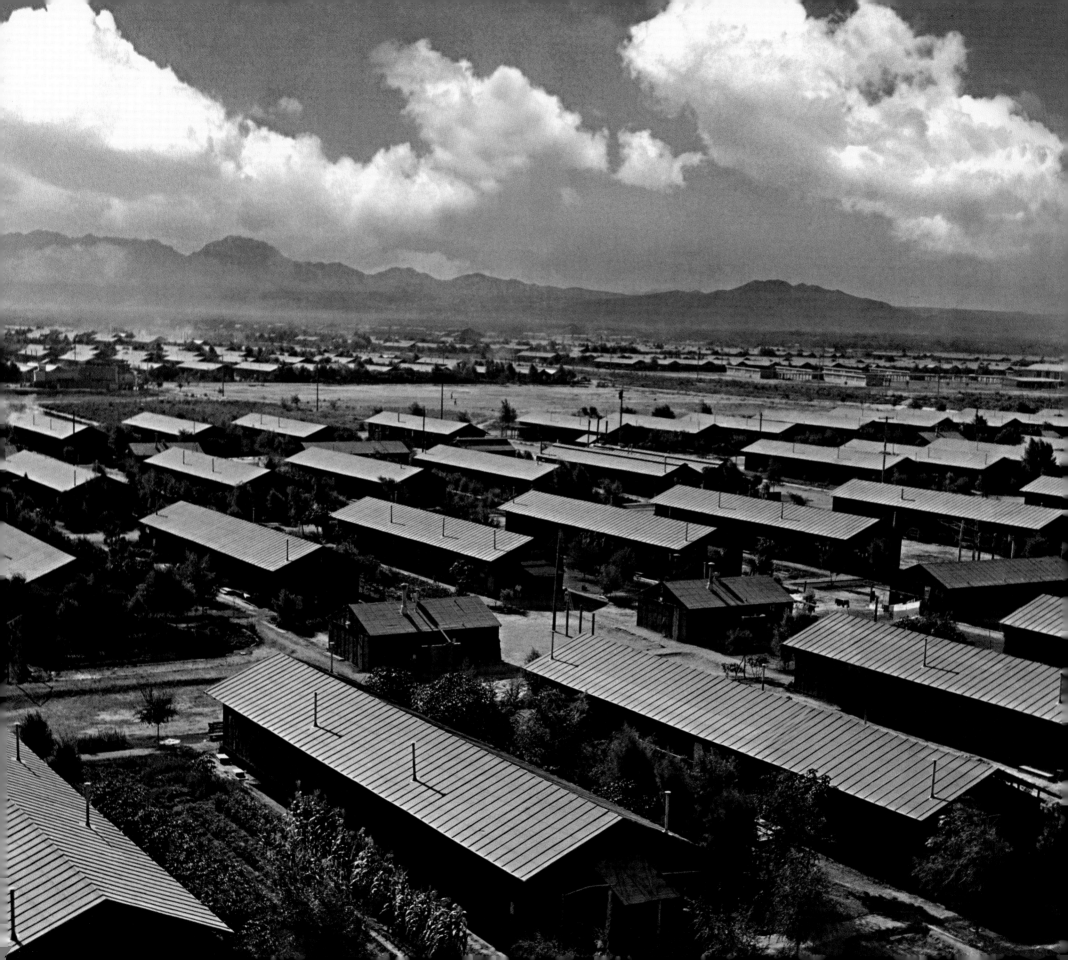

For many months we have lived in the middle of the desert in a place called Manzanar. Miles and miles of barbed wire surround us, like weeds on a vine, growing from the hate of those who have sent us here. Beyond this barren land, the world has left no place for us.

Sometimes the wind blows and blows, and it feels as if we will blow away with it.

Everyone tries their best to make this place a home.

On land that once was dry and cracked, now there lies a baseball field.

In Manzanar we do not have much, but we still save our pennies, nickels, and dimes to buy war bonds to support our country. We pull together to contribute what little we have to America. How strange that we support our country from behind its prison walls.

Mothers and fathers bid their sons farewell. Just one last glimpse to say goodbye as they ride away in the back of a military truck. Beyond the barbed wire they go to fight for America, the country they believe in. One day things will be better.

In school we pledge allegiance to the one and only flag of our only country. We are still Americans, though no one else thinks so.

Everyone tries to forget that we are behind barbed wire. But it is hard to pretend that we do not see the guard towers and the soldiers with guns. It is hard to pretend that we are not home. Forgetting is not an easy thing to do.

Grandfather tells me that the desert is a beautiful place, but all I see is dust that stings the eye. How can I find beauty where there seems to be none?

"Look beyond the barbed wire," Grandfather says to me. "Look beyond the barbed wire, and you will begin to see."

The snow covered mountains outside our door stretch on for miles and miles.

At night I see the sky as clear as can be. The stars shine bright and unafraid. The unrelenting wind brings the cry of a lonely coyote. Grandfather is right, the desert is a beautiful place.

In the next barrack there lived a kind lady named Ryo. Last night she passed away, she was very, very sick. She left before the morning came to join the other stars in the sky. There she will shine bright and unafraid. There she will be free. With prayer and flowers we will say goodbye.

But flowers do not grow in the desert. Paper scraps are gathered. Grandmothers, aunts, mothers, and daughters sit down at the same table. They take the paper in their hands and silently they work. To the paper they tell the secrets of their hearts and the flowers begin to bloom. From the ordinary comes something beautiful.

Each flower is a silent tribute to the unspoken camaraderie we share. It means we understand the loss of all that is gone.

Everything is in between. In between happiness and sorrow. In between how things were, and how they will turn out. Our life is lived in between America and its freedom.

We do not know whether to laugh or cry, so we just keep on trying.

Mothers and fathers receive news about their sons who went to fight in the war. Many soldiers will not be coming home. "Bravely he went forth to die for this country," that is what the telegram says, written by military officials that did not know him.

But they never heard his laugh, they never saw his smile. They never knew his kind heart. He was America's son.

The barbed wire, the guard tower, and the desert wind seem to whisper, *bravely you have gone forth to die for this country, but we still do not want you here.*

I will fly a kite for them, for the many Japanese American soldiers who will never be able to see their families again. It will fly high and soar like their fighting spirit of courage and loyalty. It will fly beyond this place.

My kite catches the wind and soars like an eagle who has found his way home. But slowly the wind shifts. As quick as the kite rises, down to the earth it falls. It tangles in the barbed wire fence and reminds me that we are not free.

America is our only country,
but we are the only Americans
that have been forgotten.

THEN ONE DAY, UPON THE DESERT WIND WAS CARRIED THE GOOD NEWS. AT LAST THE WAR IS OVER. FOR THREE YEARS we have lived here in this place called Manzanar. Three years is a long time to have lived behind barbed wire, miles and miles from America. With hope in our eyes and faith in our hearts, we turn to one another and say, "We can go home."

The lonely desert mountains have stood each day as silent witnesses. Though they appear unchanging and seem to stay the same, they have seen that war can mean many things, like what has happened here.

We pack our whole life in one suitcase again, but at least now we are free.
We have known what it is like to walk in America's shadow.

Though we were surrounded by desolation, we breathed life into this place.

The high school kids danced as the band played on, the music rising high above the lights of this city in the dust.

From far away you could hear it, the sound of people trying their best to make the most with what America had left them. It was the sound of people trying to live as normal a life as possible on a battlefield of hate.

This place was barren, but our spirits were not.

The wind blows the dust and it beats against the side of a tar papered barrack. But now the barrack is empty. Soundless and still, this place breathes no more.

Many years from now, when time has gone by, what will become of Manzanar? The barracks, the barbed wire, the guard tower—these things do not last forever. When everything else is gone, what will remain? Will anyone know what happened here? Will anyone know what happened to us?

Who will remember the ones who walked through the barbed wire to come here, but who never walked back out again? Who will tell *our* story?

Then I remembered what Grandfather
had told me, that one day I would find
a way to help. Finally, I knew how.

Maybe one day when I am all grown up, a child will come and ask me what it means to be an American. I will remember this time and place and people, and I will tell their stories.

I will tell this child a story about a place called Manzanar, and how we were like those desert stars who shine bright even though it is dark.

I will tell this child that you cannot imprison a spirit that refuses to be imprisoned.

This is the promise I make to keep the past alive. To honor those who lived through it, and to honor those who died because of it. This is something I can do for them.

I look into my grandfather's eyes and deep down in my heart I understand. America is still a good place. It is still a good place because in our own way we have helped to make it so.

Grandfather takes my hand in his and together we walk beyond the barbed wire.

TOO PAINFUL TO REMEMBER,

TOO IMPORTANT TO EVER FORGET

"RACE PREJUDICE, WAR HYSTERIA, AND A FAILURE OF POLITICAL LEADERSHIP." These were the words used by a presidential commission in the 1980s to describe the reasons for the exclusion and incarceration of Japanese Americans during World War II. All individuals of Japanese ancestry were excluded and forcibly removed from the West Coast region of the United States. Those who did not leave the area soon enough were incarcerated in concentration camps scattered across the country. In total, over 110,000 persons were kept in these camps for up to four years. Nearly two-thirds of these individuals were American citizens by birth. Of those who were not American citizens, most had lived the majority of their lives in the United States, but were prohibited by anti-Asian laws from becoming citizens.

IN AMERICA'S SHADOW TELLS THIS STORY IN A VERY PERSONAL AND POIGNANT WAY. The story of what happened to Japanese Americans during World War II is one of devastating loss and struggle; but it is also one of extraordinary will and courage to persevere. It is a story which at times is too painful to remember; yet it is one much too important to ever forget.

ON DECEMBER 7, 1941, JAPAN ATTACKED PEARL HARBOR, A U.S. NAVAL HARBOR in the U.S. Territory of Hawai`i. The United States was immediately thrust into the Pacific Theater of World War II. Anti-Japanese sentiment had been growing for several decades in the United States, particularly in the western states. The attack on Pearl Harbor, preceded by years of anti-Japanese fervor, set off the chain of events that would lead to the incarceration of Japanese Americans.

ON FEBRUARY 19, 1942, PRESIDENT FRANKLIN D. ROOSEVELT SIGNED EXECUTIVE ORDER 9066. This order authorized the secretary of war to designate "military areas" from which "any or all persons may be excluded." While the order did not specifically identify any ethnicity, it became the foundation for the exclusion and incarceration of Japanese Americans. All of this occurred despite the fact that the Federal Bureau of Investigations, the Office of Naval Intelligence, and the Federal Communications Commission all informed President Roosevelt that Japanese Americans posed no security threat.

THE U.S. GOVERNMENT MOVED QUICKLY IN ESTABLISHING PLANS AND PROCEDURES for the removal of Japanese Americans from the West Coast. Government notices were posted instructing all Japanese Americans to leave their homes and take only a minimal amount of belongings. Individuals lost their homes, their businesses, their jobs, and many other material possessions. The elderly were ripped away from familiar surroundings and the stability of their homes. Children had to say goodbye to their non-Japanese American friends. Young adults, unable to finish their education, left college and other types of job training. People were forced to leave behind their pets, their friends, and their neighborhood. But perhaps the greatest loss Japanese Americans suffered, was the loss of the civil rights and liberties promised by the U.S. Constitution. These persons received no due process. There were no formal charges, no trial, and no chances for appeal — there was only guilt by ethnicity.

JAPANESE AMERICANS WERE INITIALLY SENT TO "ASSEMBLY CENTERS." Such centers were hastily arranged areas, some of which were racetrack stables that only weeks before had housed livestock. Families were forced to live in cramped quarters that reeked of animal waste. Eventually these individuals were moved to concentration camps in desert regions, swamplands, and barren, desolate areas of the United States. The camps were located in Manzanar, California; Tule Lake, California; Heart Mountain, Wyoming; Minidoka, Idaho; Rohwer, Arkansas; Jerome, Arkansas; Poston, Arizona; Gila River, Arizona; Topaz, Utah; and Amache, Colorado.

THE CAMPS WERE GENERALLY SURROUNDED BY BARBED WIRE AND MILITARY GUARD TOWERS with their guns pointed in toward the camp. The housing and food were often substandard. In many of the camps the dust penetrated the walls and floors of the crudely constructed wooden barracks. Numerous families would share a barrack, sometimes with only hanging blankets dividing their living quarters. The winters were freezing cold, and the summers unbearably hot. In these desolate areas the American dream instantly became a nightmare for Japanese Americans.

FOUR CASES WHICH PROTESTED THE TREATMENT OF JAPANESE AMERICANS reached the U.S. Supreme Court. The first three cases challenged the rights of the U.S. government to impose curfew and exclusion orders on a single ethnic group. These cases were filed by Minoru Yasui, Gordon Hirabayashi, and Fred Korematsu. In what is now considered among the gravest mistakes of the U.S. Supreme Court, the Court determined that such actions were allowable through the war powers of Congress and the president. In 1944, the Court ruled on a fourth case involving Mitsuye Endo. In this case, the Court ruled that the War Relocation Authority did not have the authority to hold loyal American citizens indefinitely without charging them with being in violation of the law.

FROM OUT OF THIS EGREGIOUS VIOLATION OF CONSTITUTIONAL RIGHTS, arose a phenomenon unparalleled in American military history. In 1942, a segregated Japanese American military unit was created to fight in the European Theater of World War II. This military unit was originally the 100th Battalion and was eventually joined by the 442nd Regimental Combat Team. The 442nd R.C.T./100th Infantry became the most decorated American military unit of its size. Unfortunately, the majority of these medals and decorations were Purple Hearts—the honor bestowed on those wounded or killed in action. Japanese Americans also served with great distinction as members of the Military Intelligence Service in the Pacific Theater of the war, as engineers in the 1399th Engineering Battalion, and in the Women's Army Corps. Despite the irony that many of the families of these individuals were behind barbed wire, these young Japanese Americans served the United States with great loyalty and courage.

AS THE CAMPS CLOSED IN 1945 AND 1946, JAPANESE AMERICANS WERE FACED with the arduous task of rebuilding their lives. Everyday concerns such as making a living, finding decent housing, and getting an education were priorities. There was little discussion focused on the obtaining of reparations, and it was not until the late 1980s that the United States government acknowledged this violation of constitutional rights.

ON AUGUST 10, 1988, PRESIDENT RONALD W. REAGAN SIGNED THE CIVIL LIBERTIES ACT which provided Japanese Americans with a presidential apology, monetary redress, and a community education fund. At the bill signing President Reagan commented, "We gather here today to right a grave wrong . . . . . no payment can make up for those lost years. So, what is most important in this bill has less to do with property than with honor. For here we admit a wrong; here we reaffirm our commitment as a nation to equal justice under the law . . . . . the ideal of liberty and justice for all—that is still the American way."

BY 1998, OVER EIGHTY-TWO THOUSAND JAPANESE AMERICANS had received an apology and monetary redress. The apology and monetary redress were just one step in the healing process for the Japanese American community and for American society. It was an act of acknowledgement, apology and atonement. As such, it was a step out of America's Shadow.

MITCHELL T. MAKI

The name *Aiko* is pronounced I-ko.
The word *keizu* is pronounced Kay-zoo.
The name *Ryo* is pronounced Ree-yo.

GLOSSARY

barbed wire Twisted strands of fence wire with sharp points.

barracks Buildings usually made of wood and tar paper that were constructed in the internment camps to house Japanese Americans.

Executive Order 9066 An order signed by President Franklin D. Roosevelt on February 19, 1942, which allowed the military to exclude any person from any area. As a result of this order, all persons of Japanese ancestry living on the west coast were forced from their homes and sent to live in internment camps.

guard tower A tall wooden structure where soldiers with guns would keep watch over the internment camp.

injustice An unfair or wrong act.

internment camp A detention center where Japanese Americans were confined during World War II. There were ten internment camps located in isolated regions of the United States.

Manzanar One of the ten internment camps. Manzanar was located in the desert of eastern California at the base of the Sierra Nevada.

war bond A certificate issued by the government as a way to borrow money from its citizens during a time of war. People could purchase war bonds to help support their country and would be paid back with interest at a later date.

World War II A war fought from 1939 to 1945, in which the Allied forces (including Britain, France, and the United States) defeated the Axis powers (including Germany, Italy and Japan).

PICTURE CREDITS

Front Cover: Komatsu Family Collection. **Back Cover:** Library of Congress, Prints & Photographs Division, Historic American Buildings Survey. i: Komatsu Family Collection. ii-iii: National Archives. v: Komatsu Family Collection. 1: Komatsu Family Collection. 3: Komatsu Family Collection. 5: Komatsu Family Collection. 7: Photo collage: Komatsu Family Collection; Library of Congress, Prints & Photographs Division, McManus-Young Collection. 9: Komatsu Family Collection. 11: Komatsu Family Collection. 13: Japanese American National Museum, gift of the Nagano Family, 93.72.357. 15: Photo collage: Komatsu Family Collection; The Fred Hultstrand History in Pictures Collection, North Dakota Institute for Regional Studies, NDSU, Fargo, ND. 16: Komatsu Family Collection. 17: (Top) National Archives; (Bottom) Seattle Post-Intelligencer Collection, Museum of History & Industry. 19: Photo collage: Komatsu Family Collection; The Fred Hultstrand History in Pictures Collection, North Dakota Institute for Regional Studies, NDSU, Fargo, ND. 21: Komatsu Family Collection. 23: Komatsu Family Collection, photograph by Norman Sugimoto. 25: Seattle Post-Intelligencer Collection, Museum of History & Industry. 27: Komatsu Family Collection. 28: Franklin D. Roosevelt Library. 29: Library of Congress, Prints & Photographs Division, FSA/OWI Collection. 31: Komatsu Family Collection. 32: National Archives. 33: Komatsu Family Collection. 34: Komatsu Family Collection. 35: Photo collage: Komatsu Family Collection; Western History Collections, University of Oklahoma Library, Campbell 1667. 37: Photo collage: Komatsu Family Collection; Library of Congress, Prints & Photographs Division, Detroit Publishing Company Collection. 39: Komatsu Family Collection. 40: Denver Public Library, Western History Collection, X-31199. 41: Denver Public Library, Western History Collection, X-31247. 43: Denver Public Library, Western History Collection, MCC-1031. 45: Komatsu Family Collection. 47: Library of Congress, Prints & Photographs Division, FSA/OWI Collection. 48: Komatsu Family Collection. 49: (Top) National Archives; (Bottom) Japanese American National Museum, Jack Iwata Photo, gift of Jack and Peggy Iwata, 93.102.163. 51: Japanese American National Museum, U.S. Army Photo, courtesy of Harold Harada, NRC.1997.94.2. 53: National Archives. 54: Japanese American National Museum, gift of Grace and George Izumi, 94.182.3. 55: Photo collage: Komatsu Family Collection; National Archives. 56-57: Komatsu Family Collection. 58: Komatsu Family Collection. 59: National Archives. 61: Komatsu Family Collection. 62: Library of Congress, Prints & Photographs Division, FSA/OWI Collection. 63: National Archives. 65: Japanese American National Museum, U.S. Army Photo, courtesy of Harold Harada, NRC.1997.94.60. 67: Collection of the Bainbridge Island Japanese American Community Photo Archives. 68: Library of Congress, Prints & Photographs Division, FSA/OWI Collection. 69: Japanese American National Museum, gift of Mary Saito Tominaga, 94.6.59E. 71: National Archives. 73: Japanese American National Museum, Jack Iwata Photo, gift of Jack and Peggy Iwata, 93.102.192. 75: Japanese American National Museum, gift of Grace and George Izumi, 94.182.9. 77: Japanese American National Museum, gift of F. Y. Hoshiyama, 96.243.3. 78: National Archives. 79: Komatsu Family Collection. 81: National Archives. 83: Japanese American National Museum, gift of Mr. and Mrs. Daisuke Kusano and family, 92.93.53. 85: National Archives. 86: Komatsu Family Collection. 87: Library of Congress, Prints & Photographs Division, photograph by Ansel Adams. 89: Komatsu Family Collection. 91: Komatsu Family Collection.
Printed in Singapore